Moonlight
Mandalas

Coloring for Adults

by

Vincent Van Gouache

Moonlight Mandalas
Coloring for Adults

The human mind has developed a unique ability to recognize patterns. It is for this reason we see animals in the clouds and beauty in the rippled sand along a deserted beach.

Relax. Breathe deeply. Let your mind clear.

Then, when you're ready, add colors that suit your mood to the patterns in this book. Let your mind wander, daydream.

A creative spirit exists in each of us. Embrace it. — Vincent

ISBN-13: 978-1533368478
ISBN-10: 1533368473

INDEX

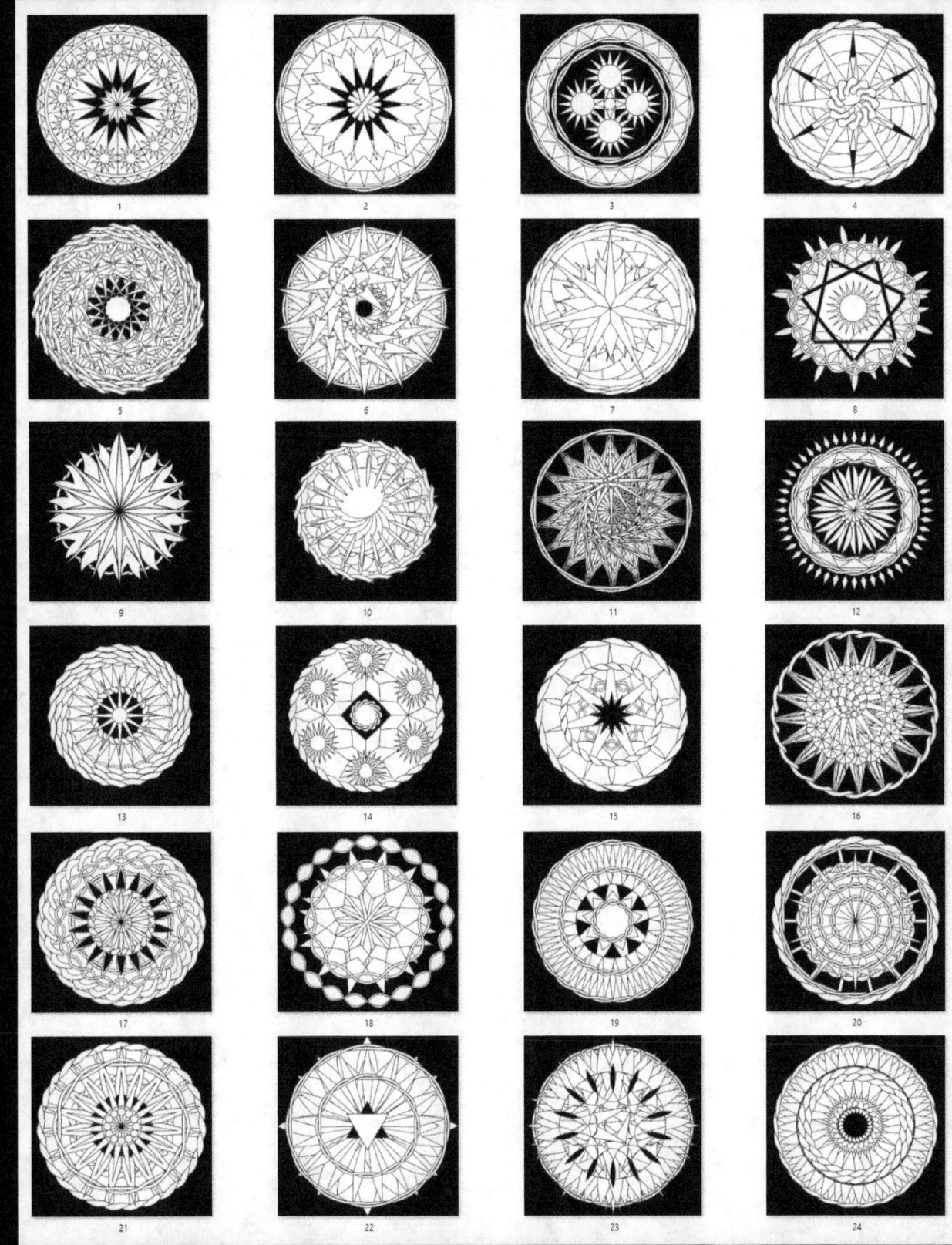

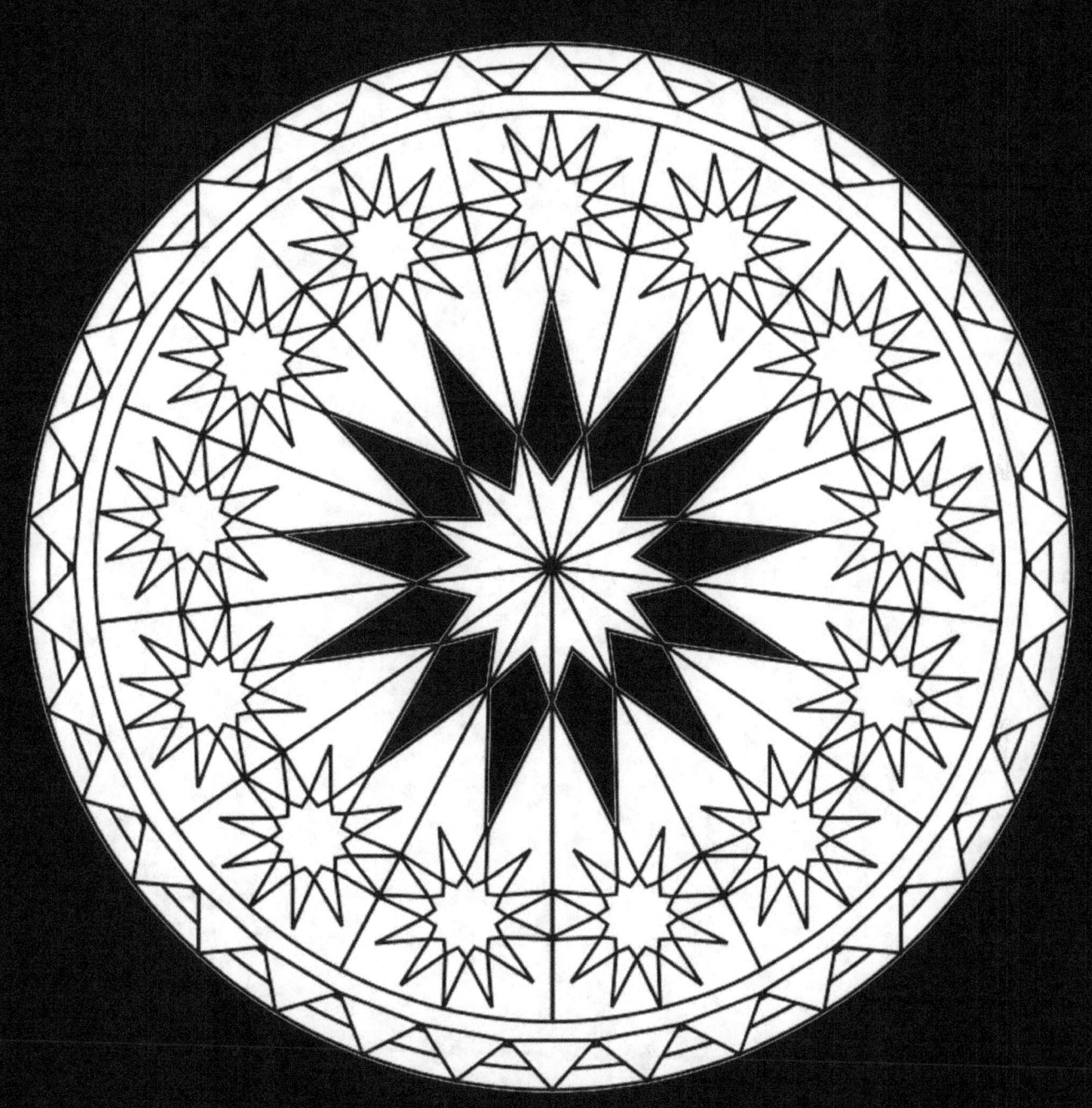

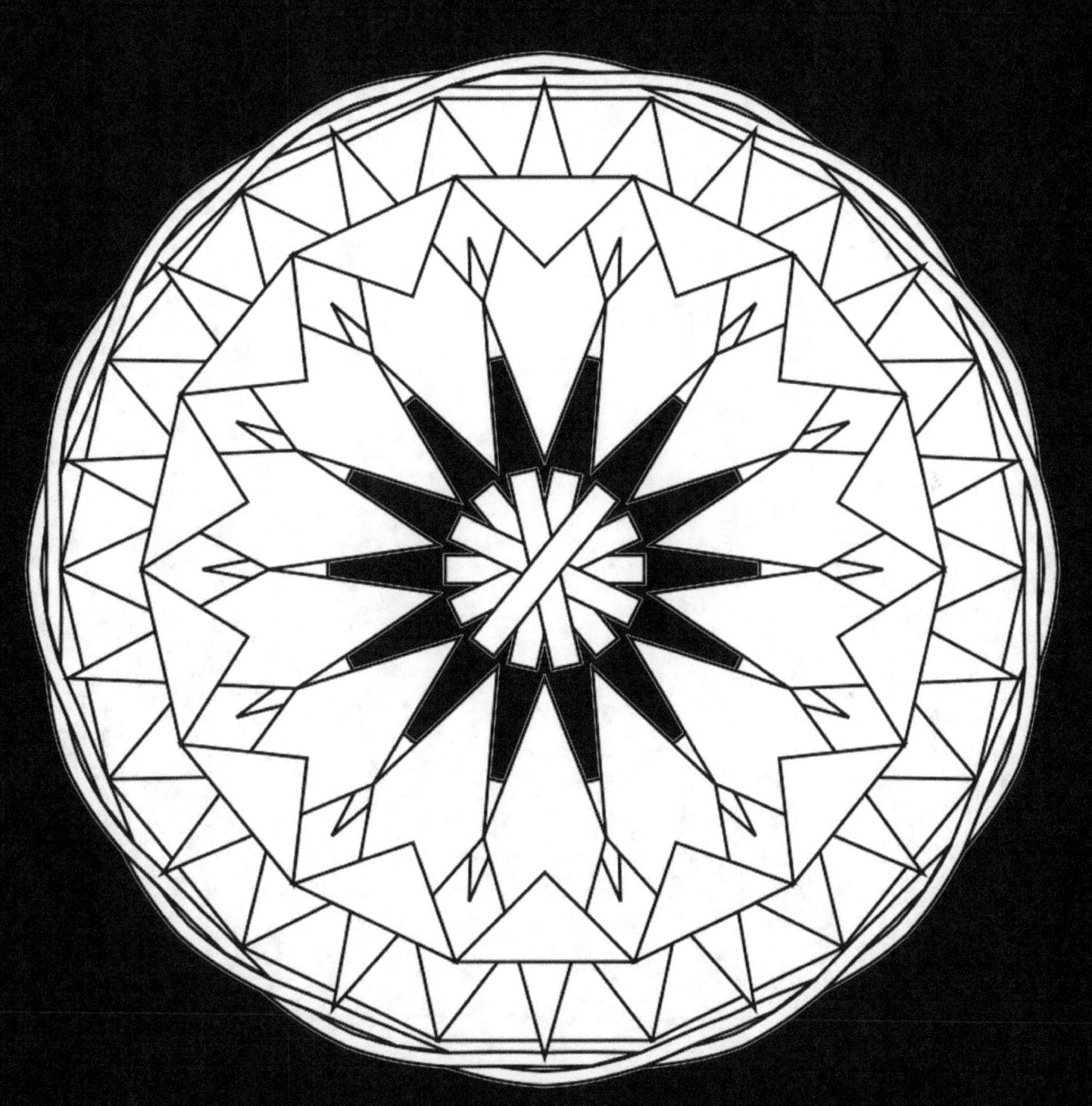

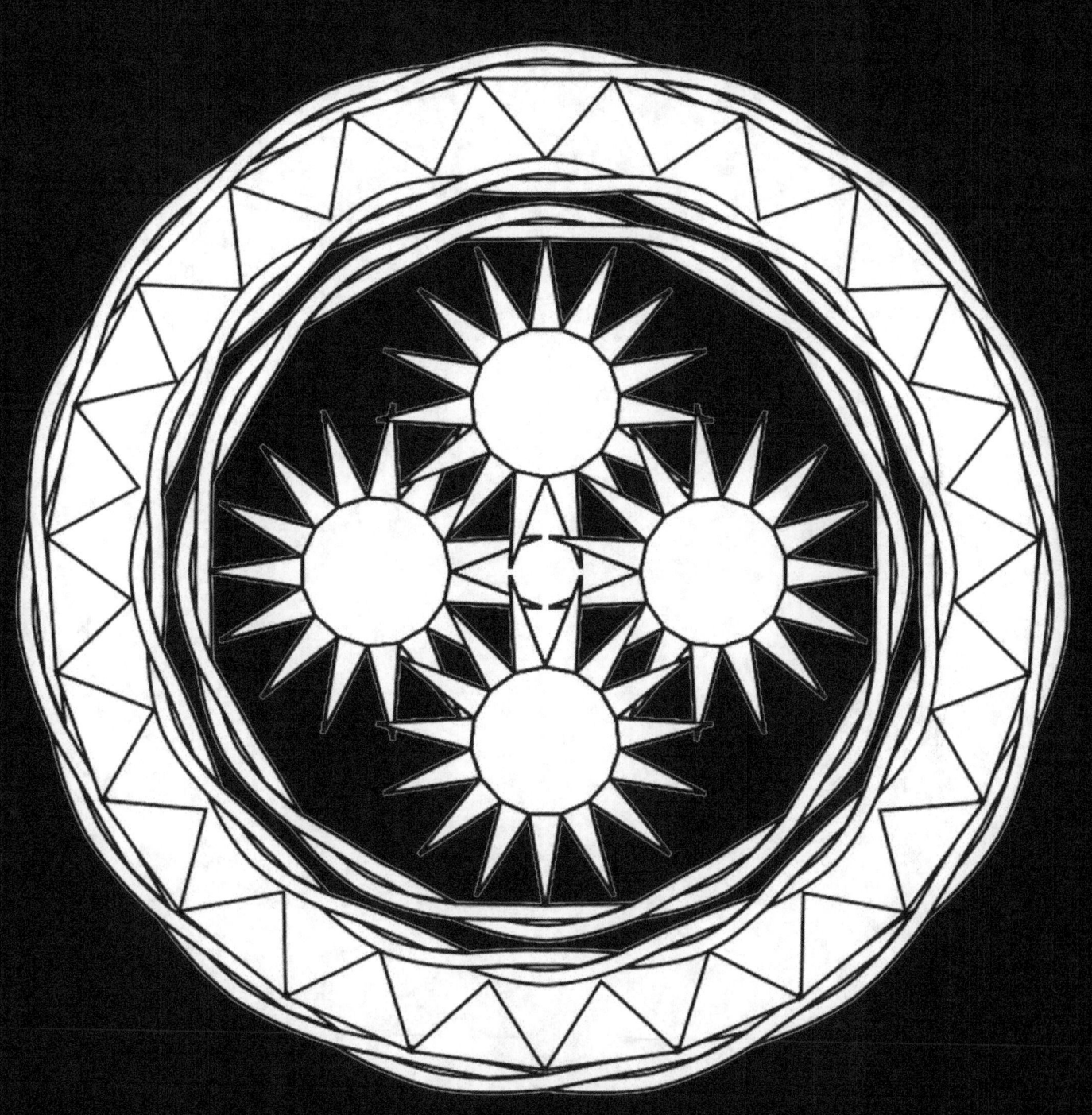

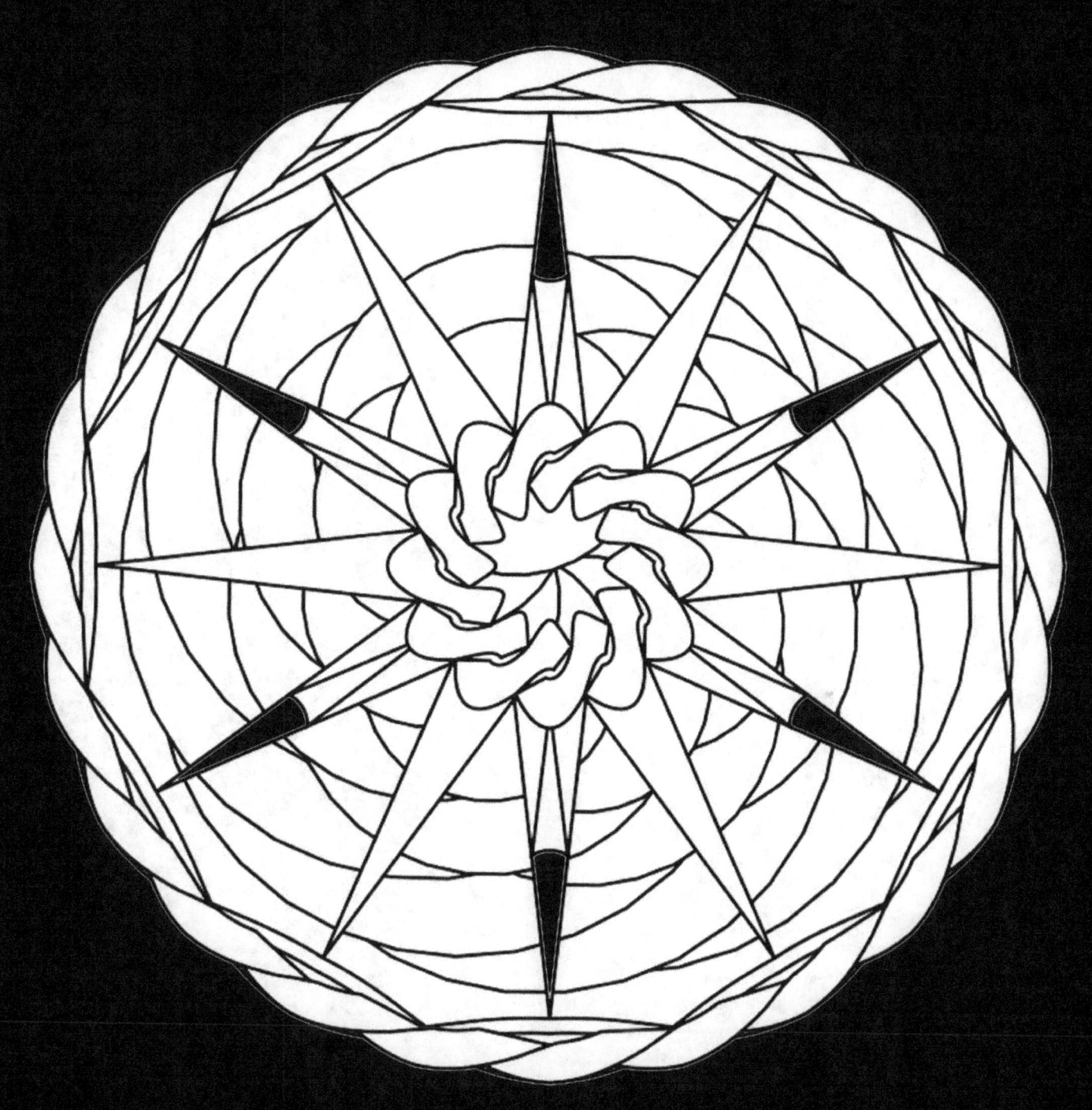

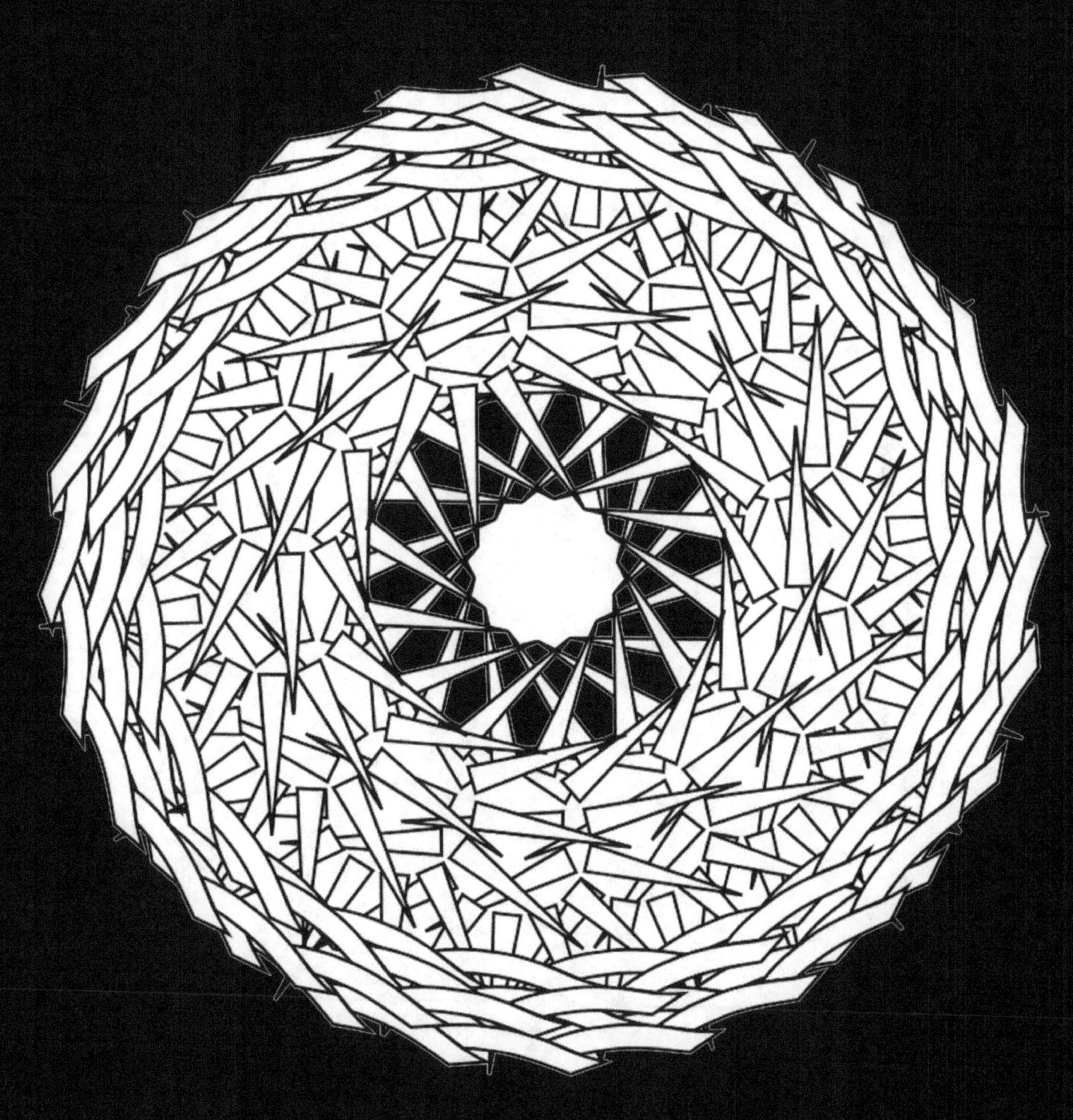

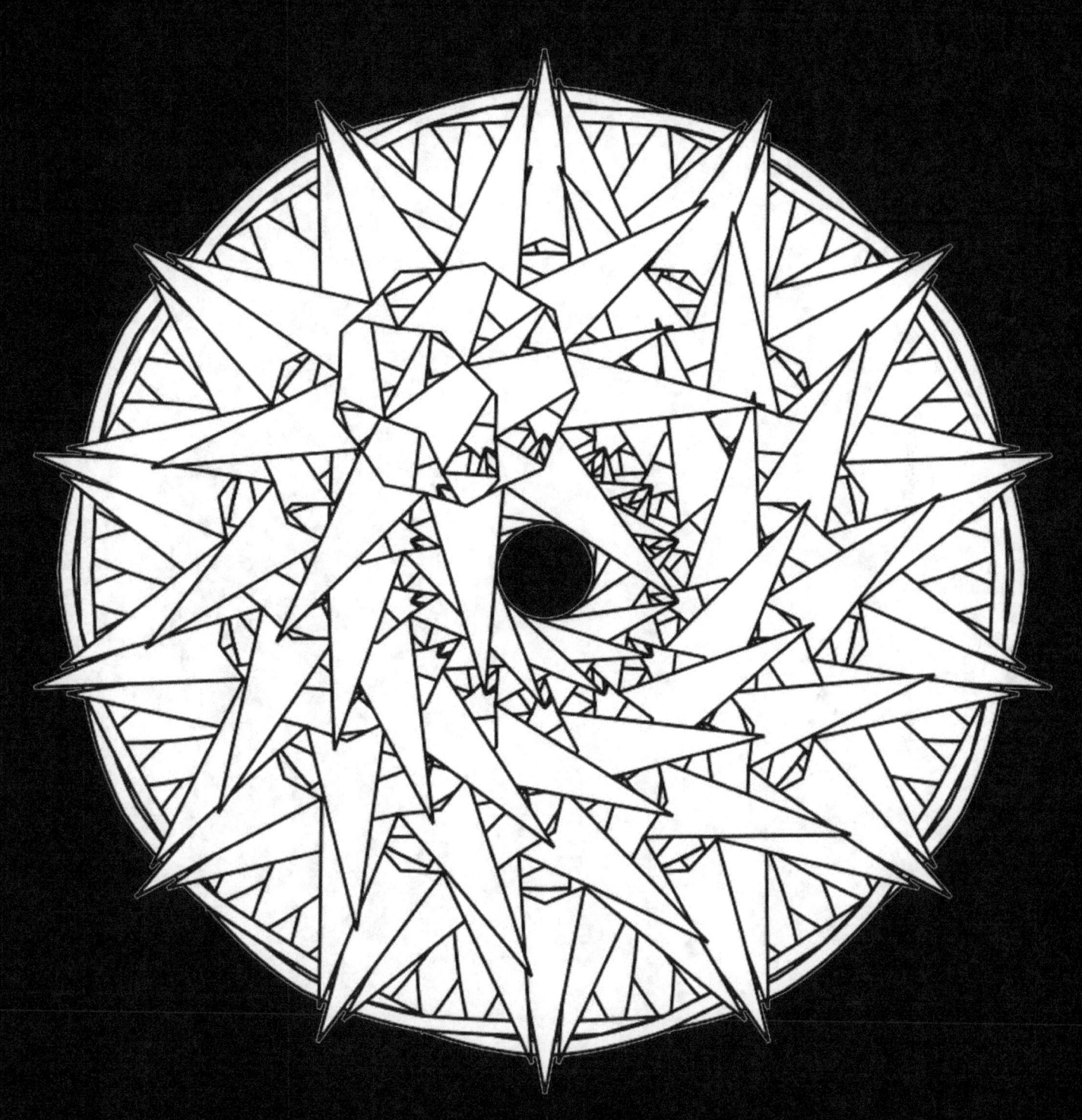

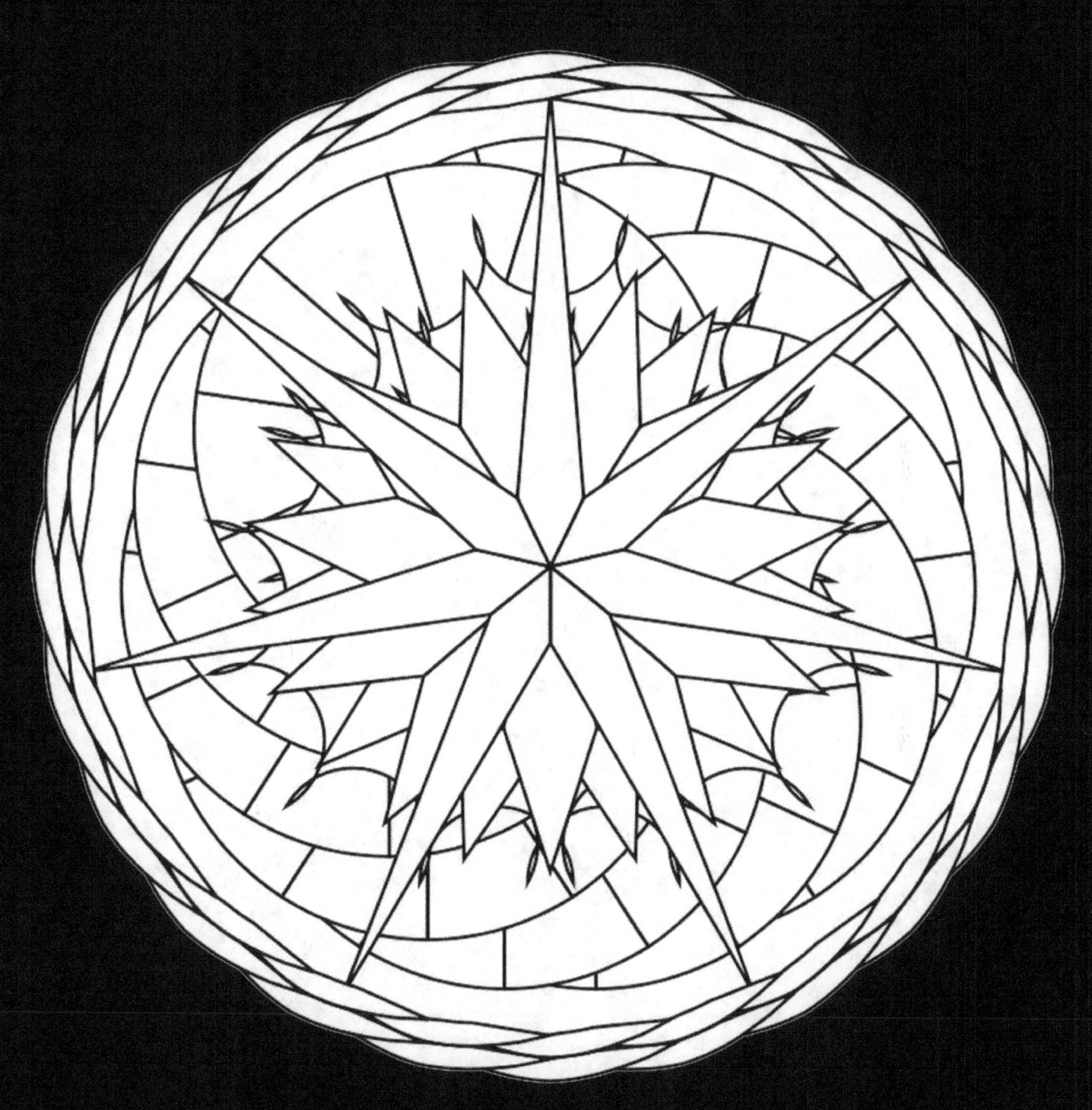

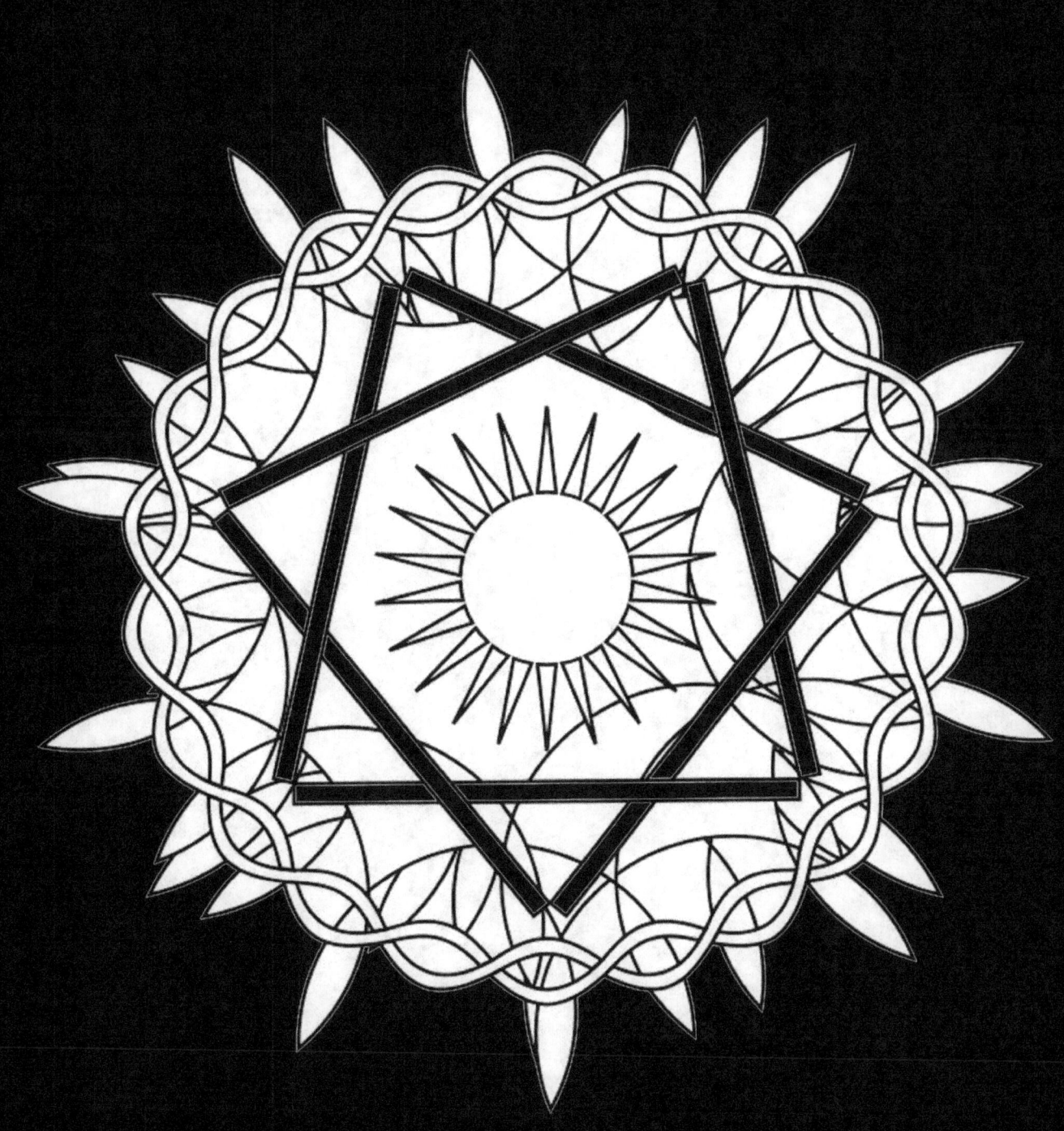

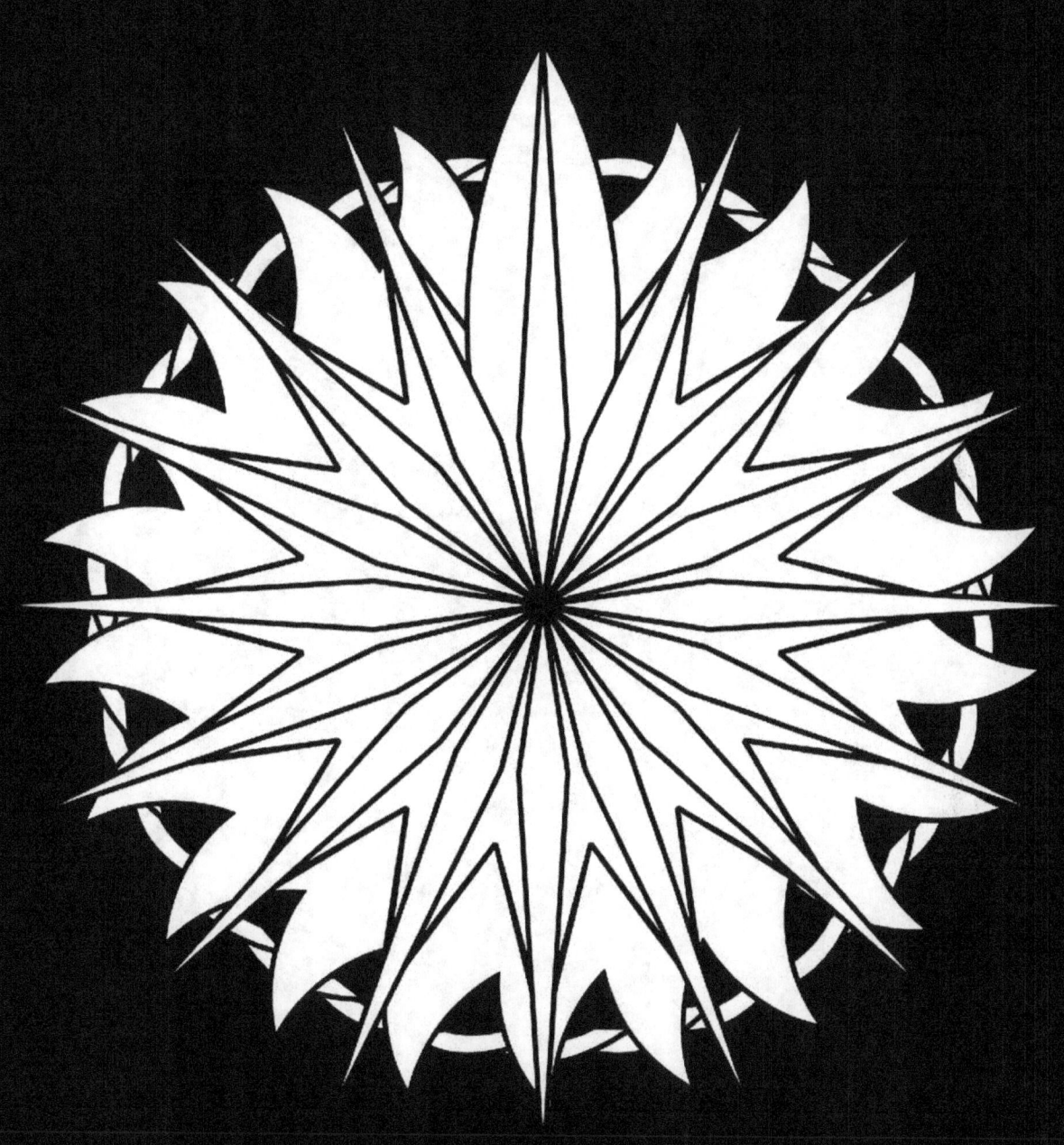

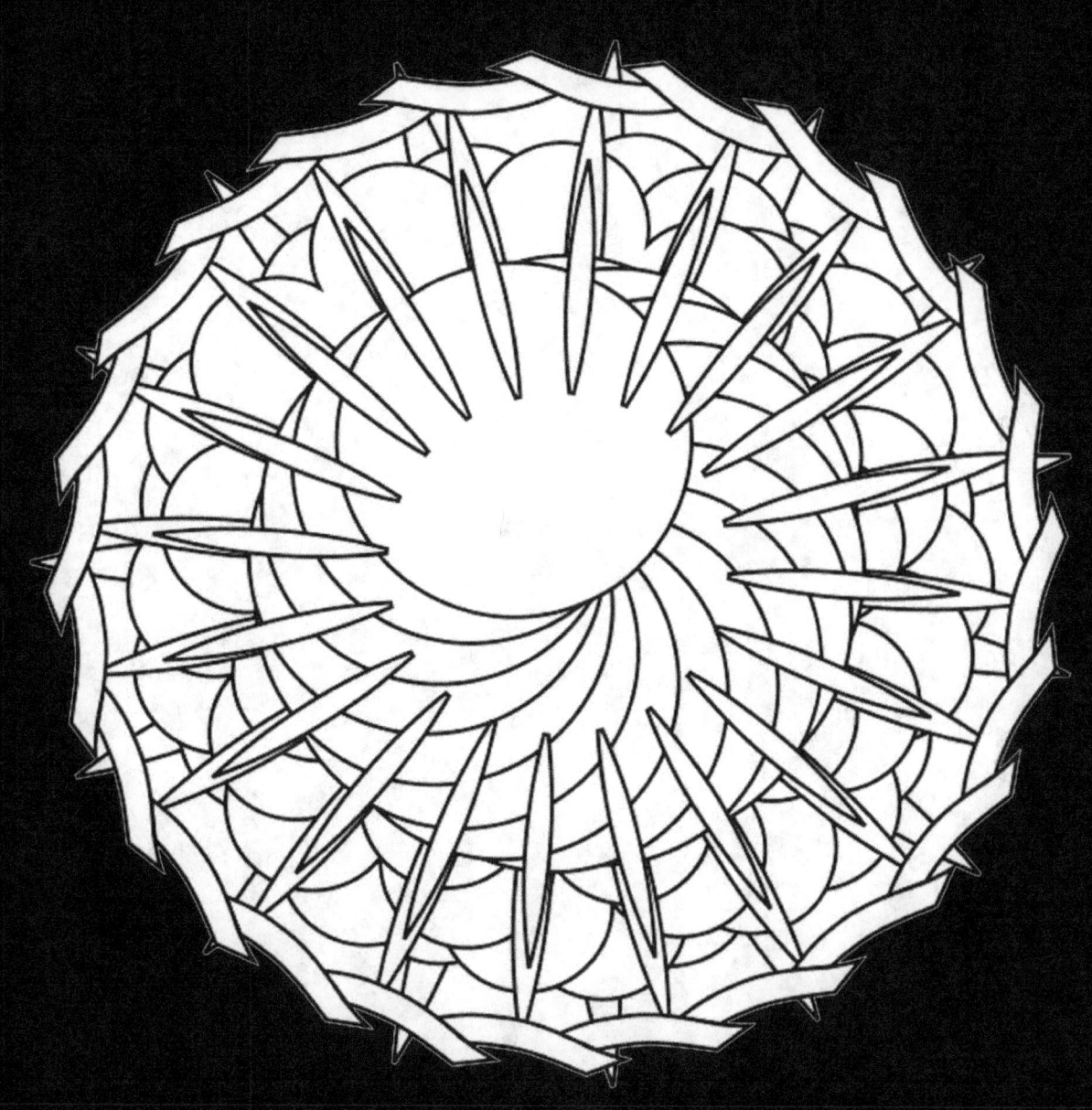

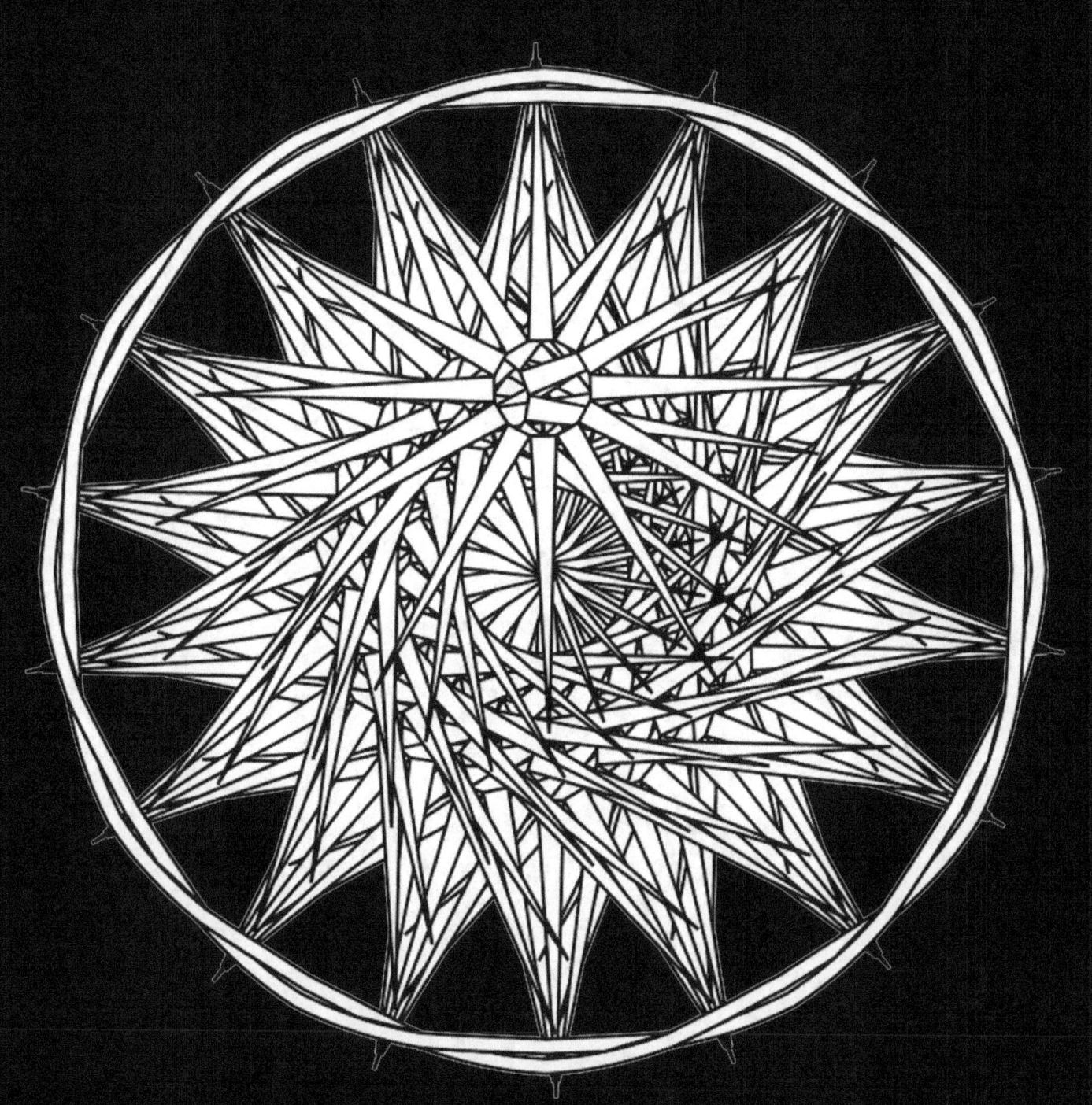

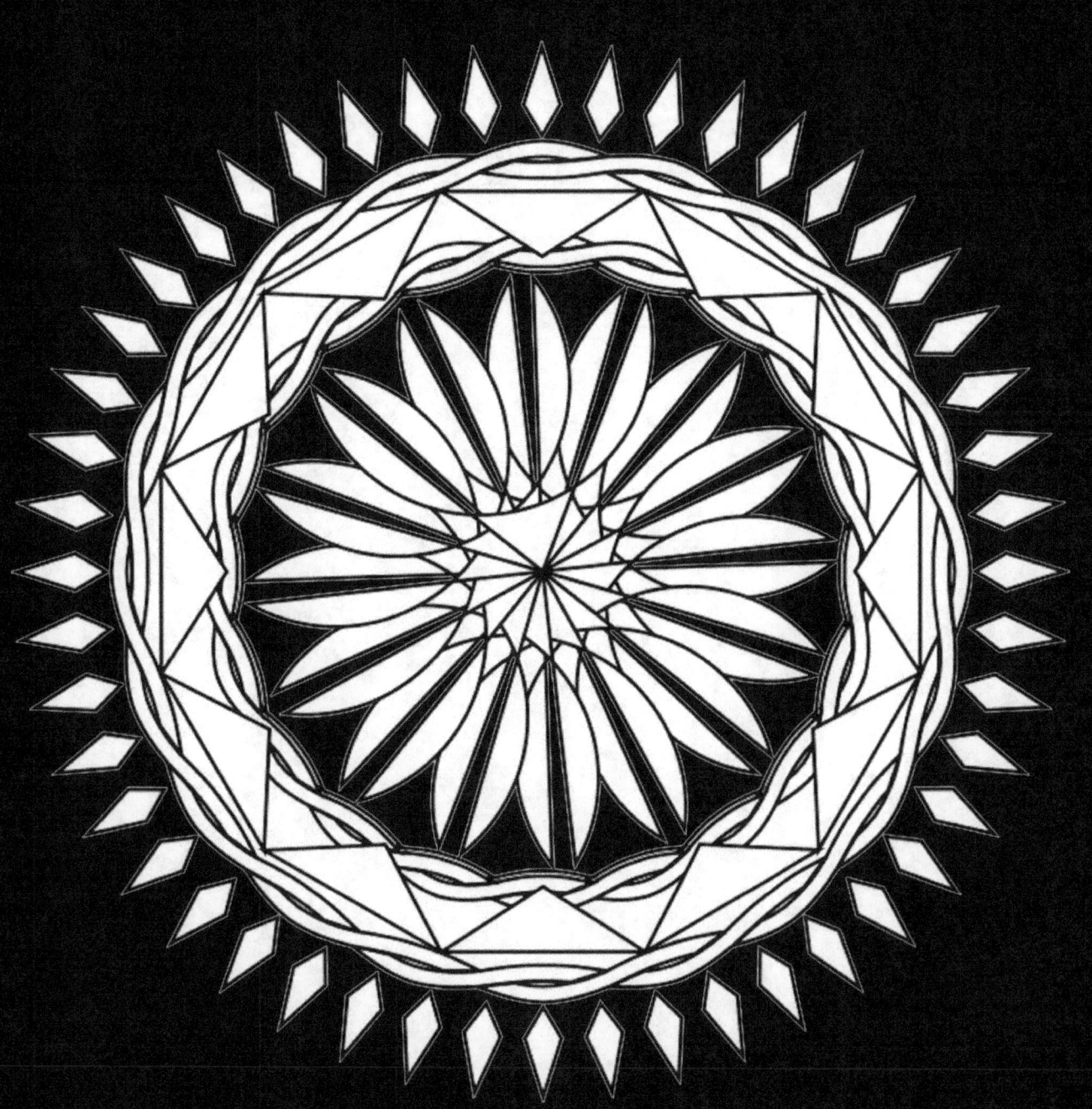

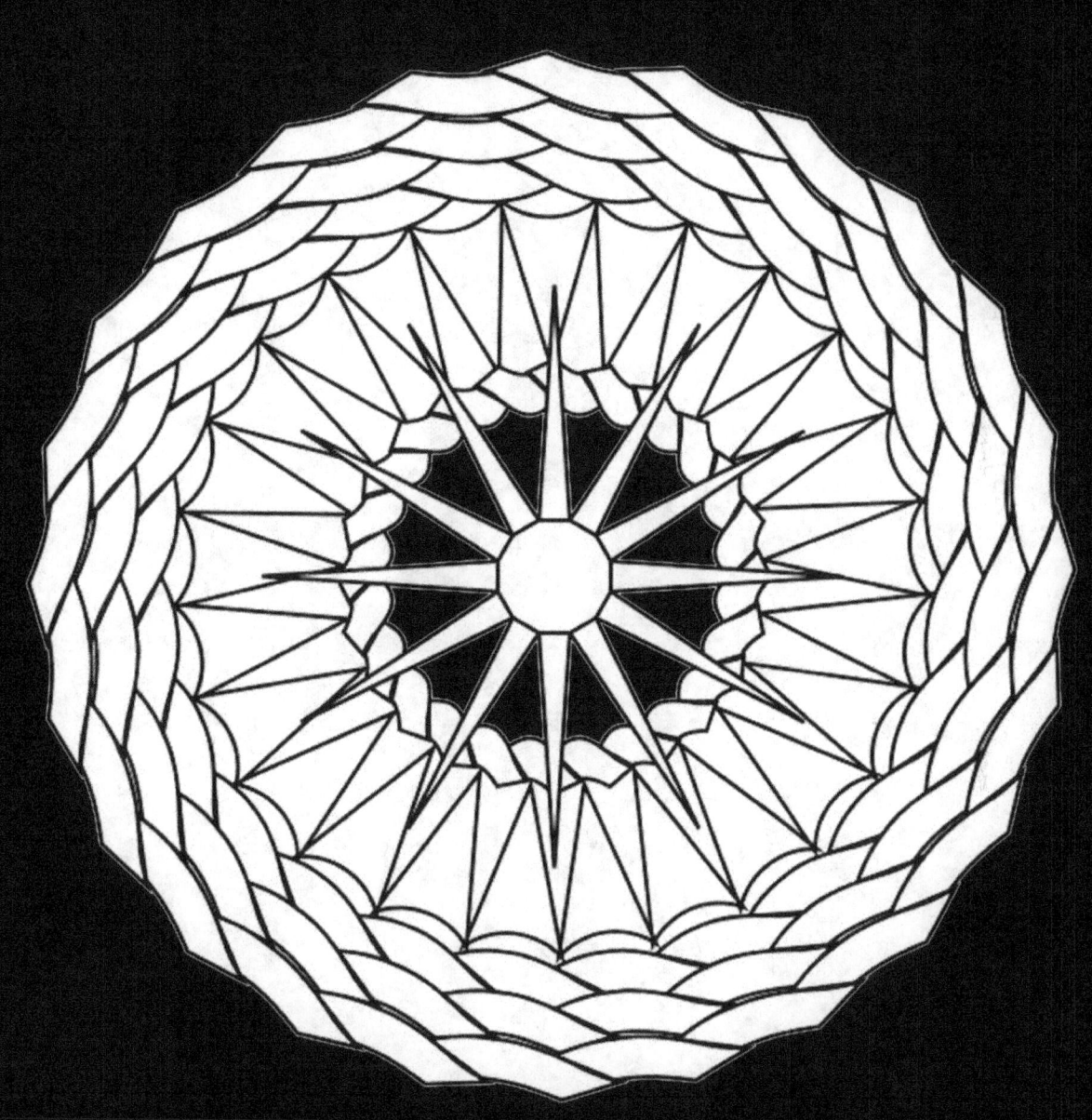

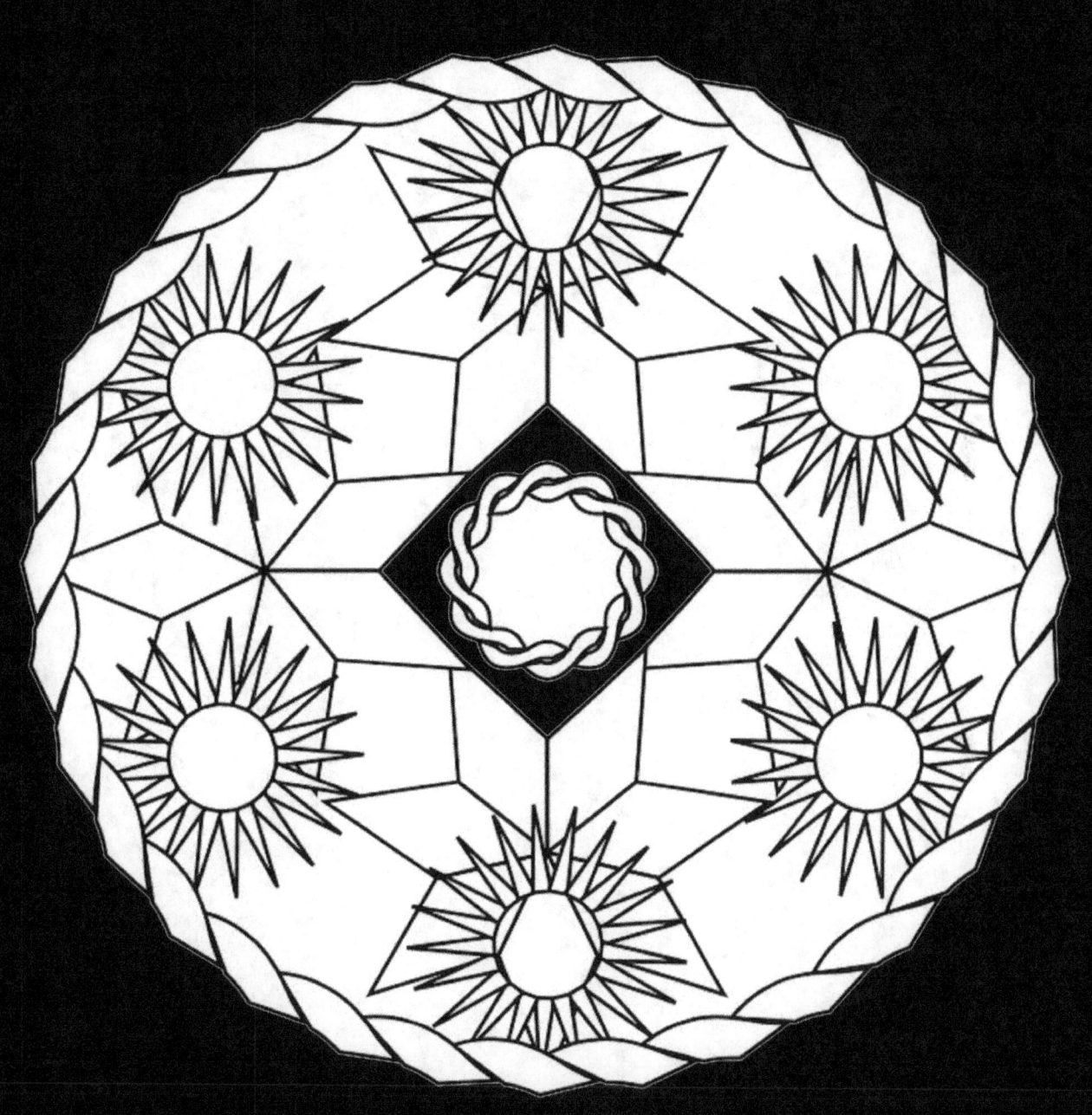

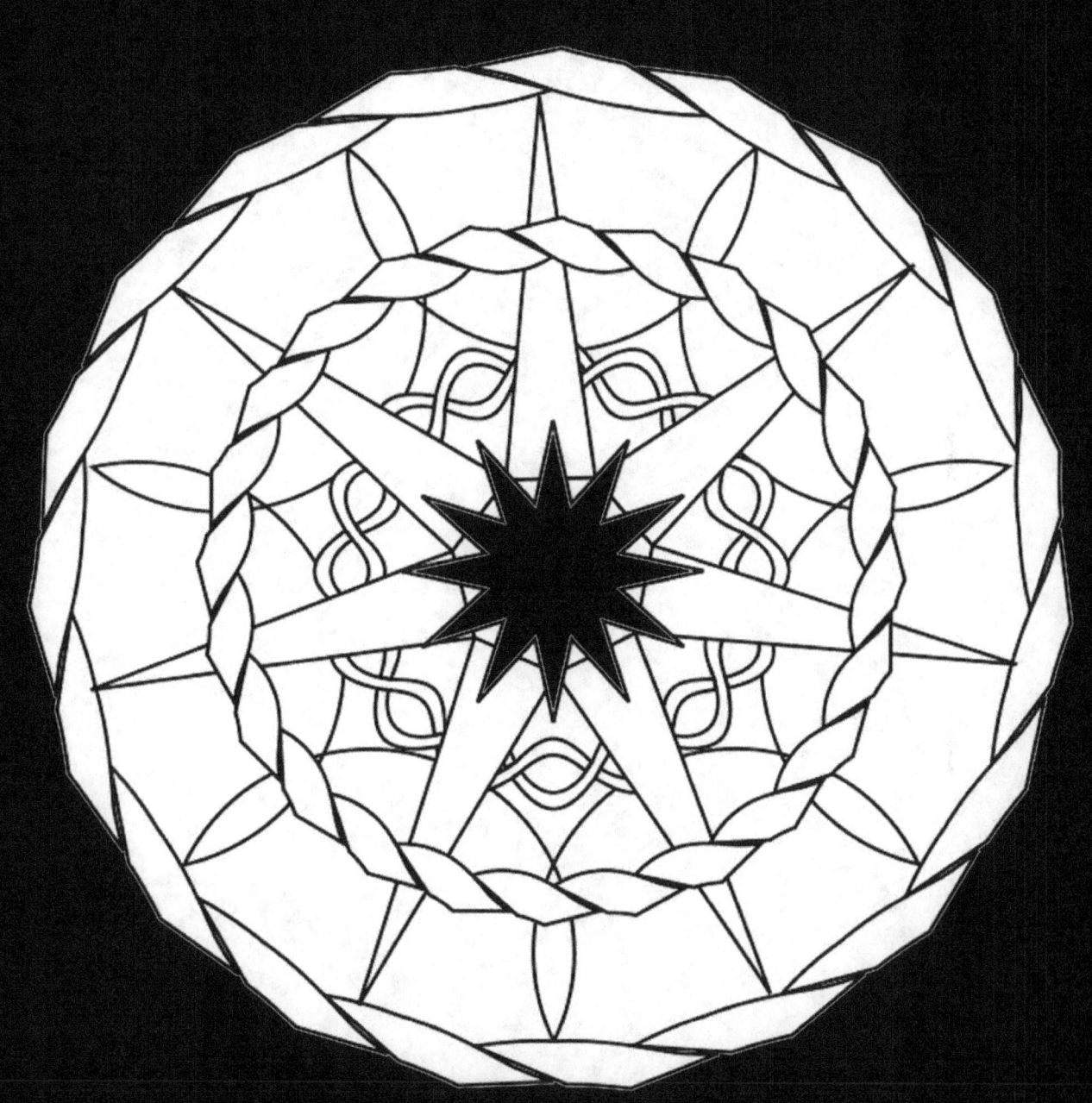

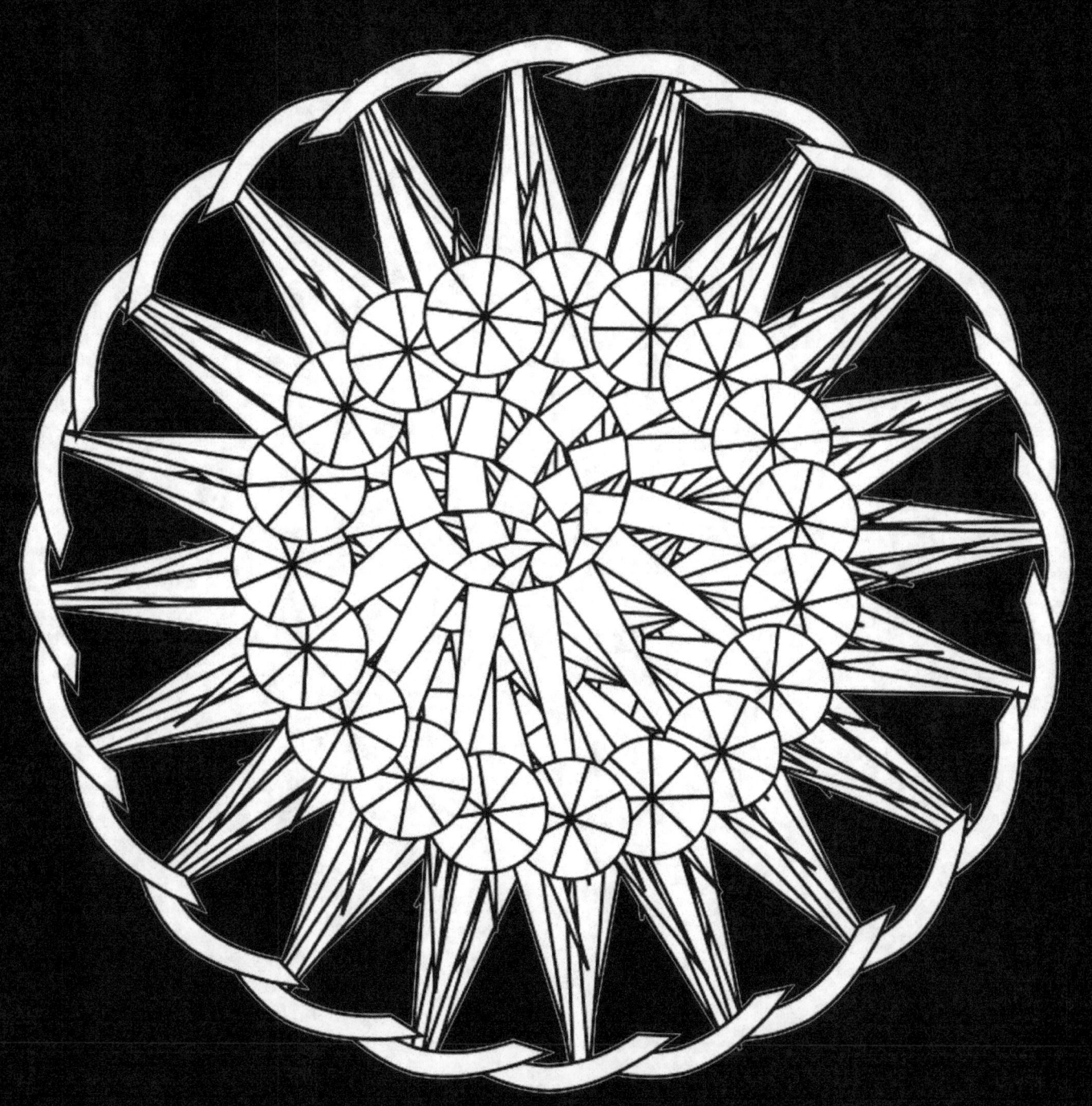

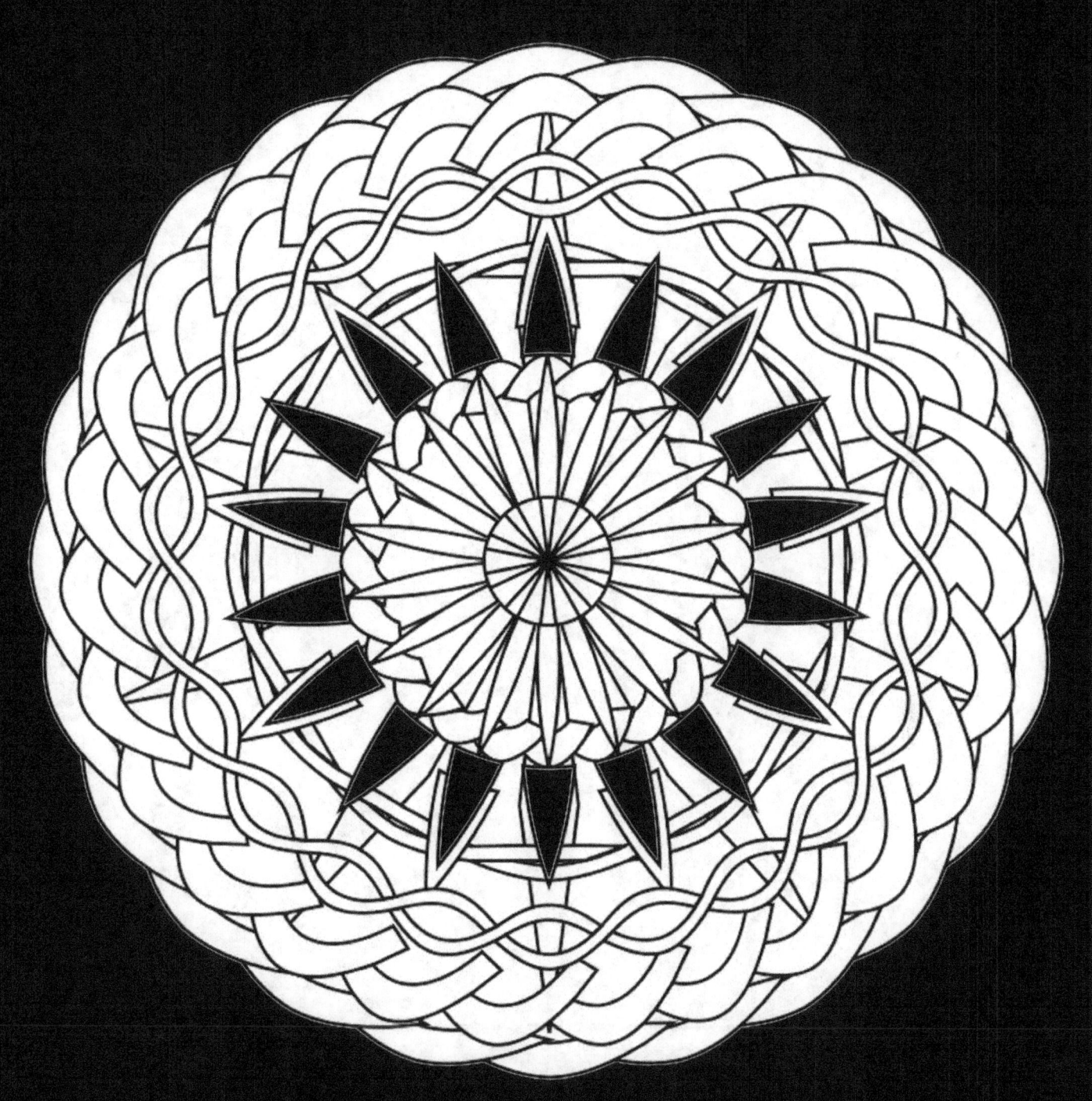

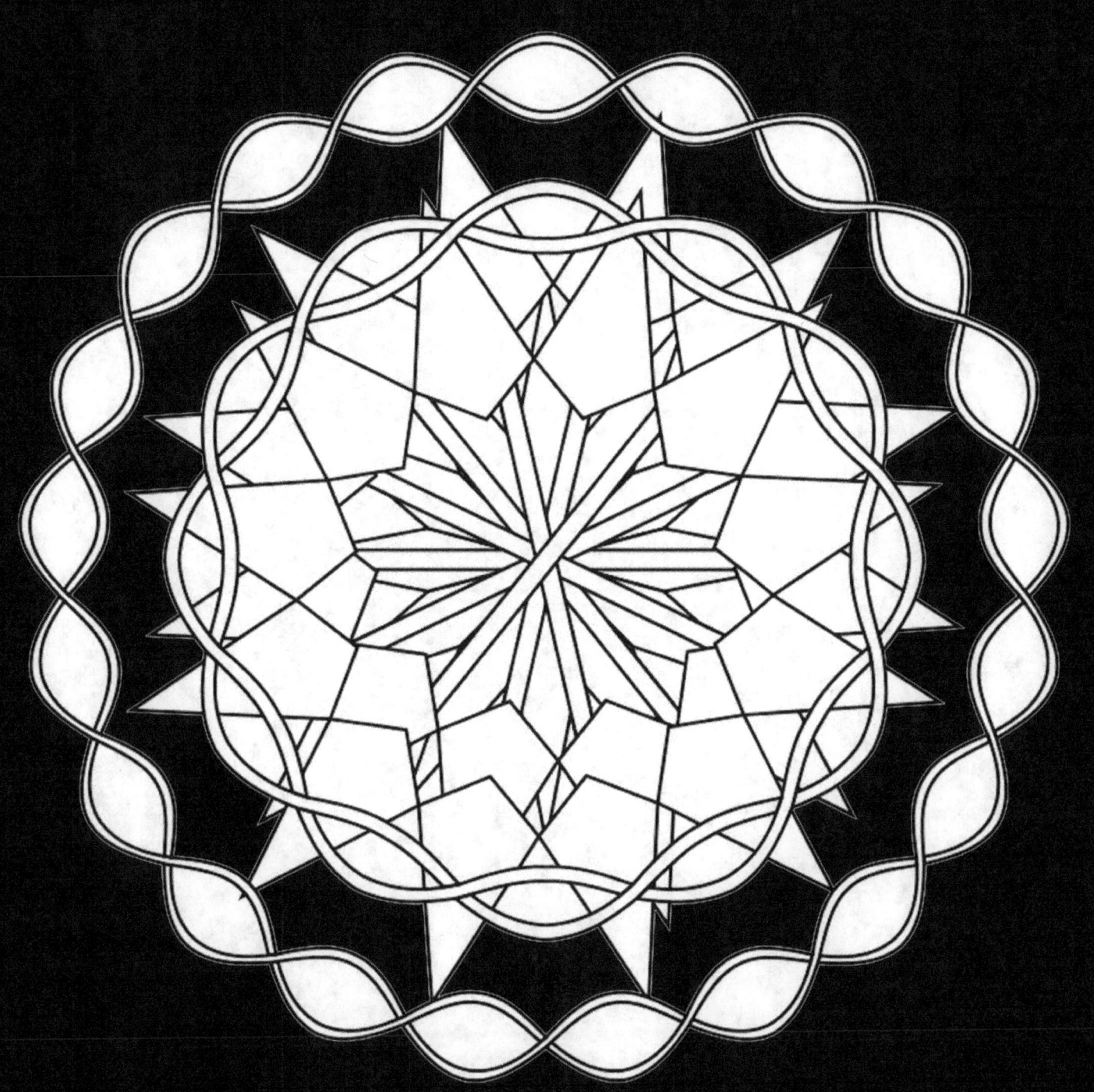

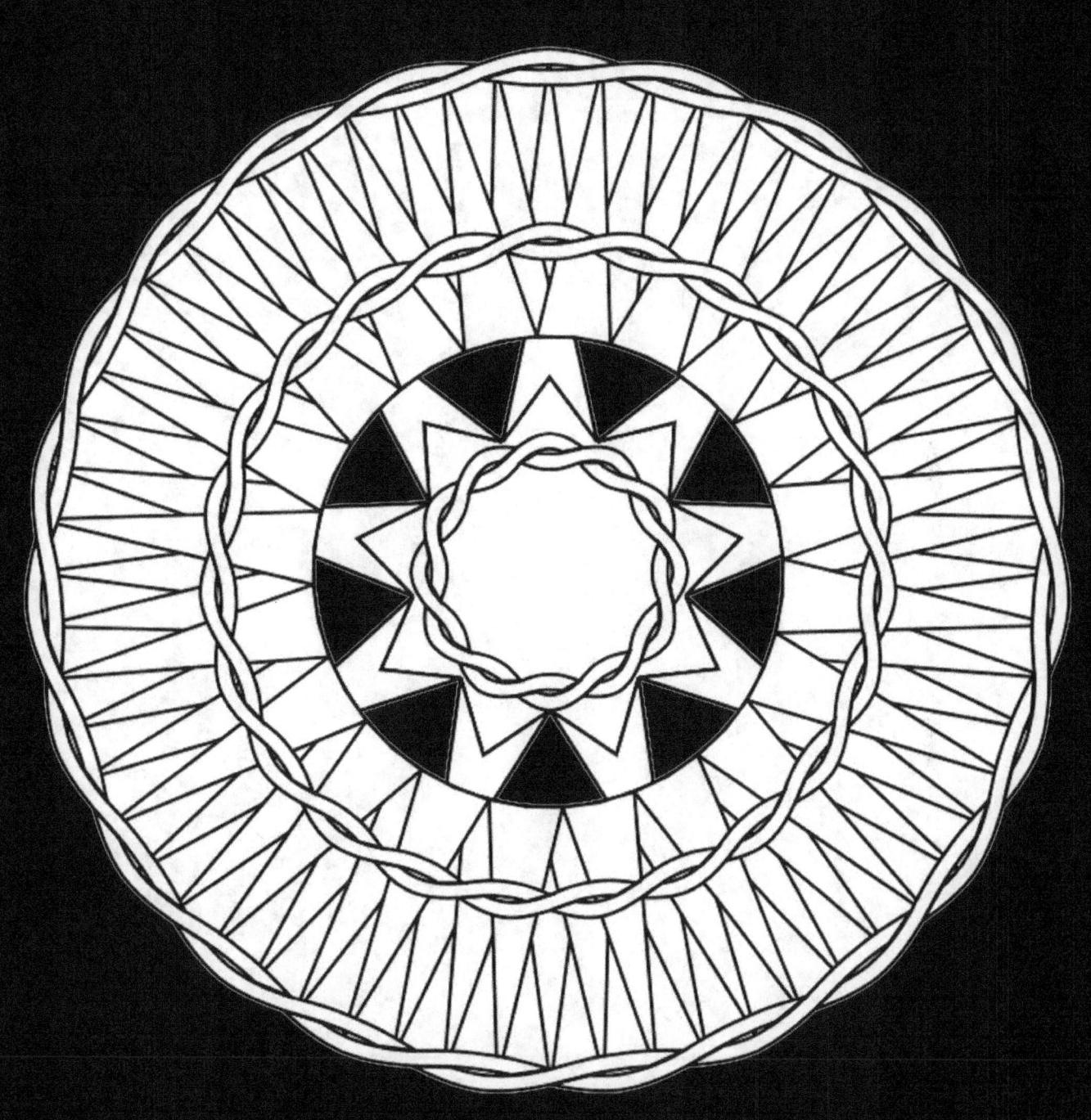

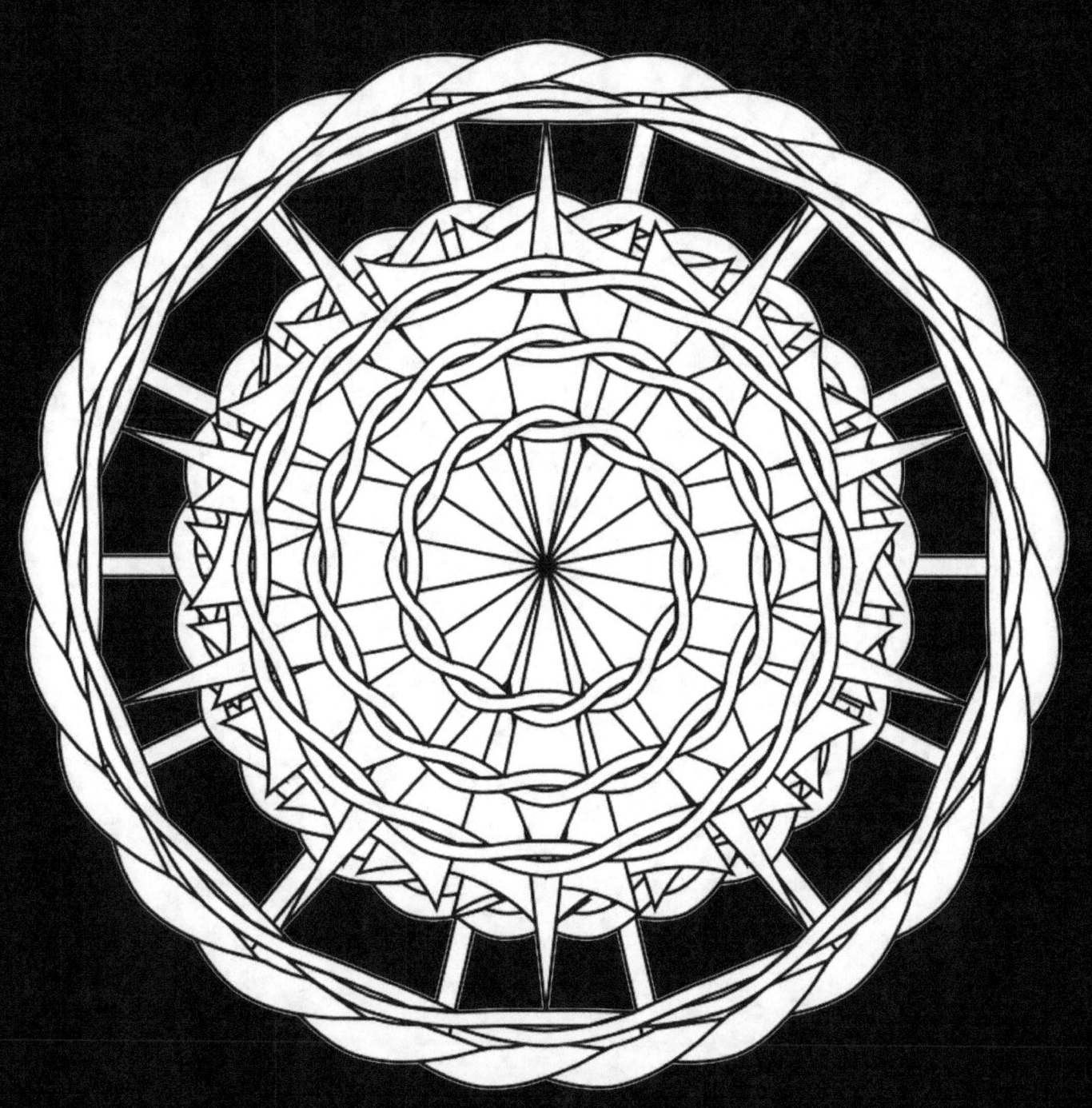

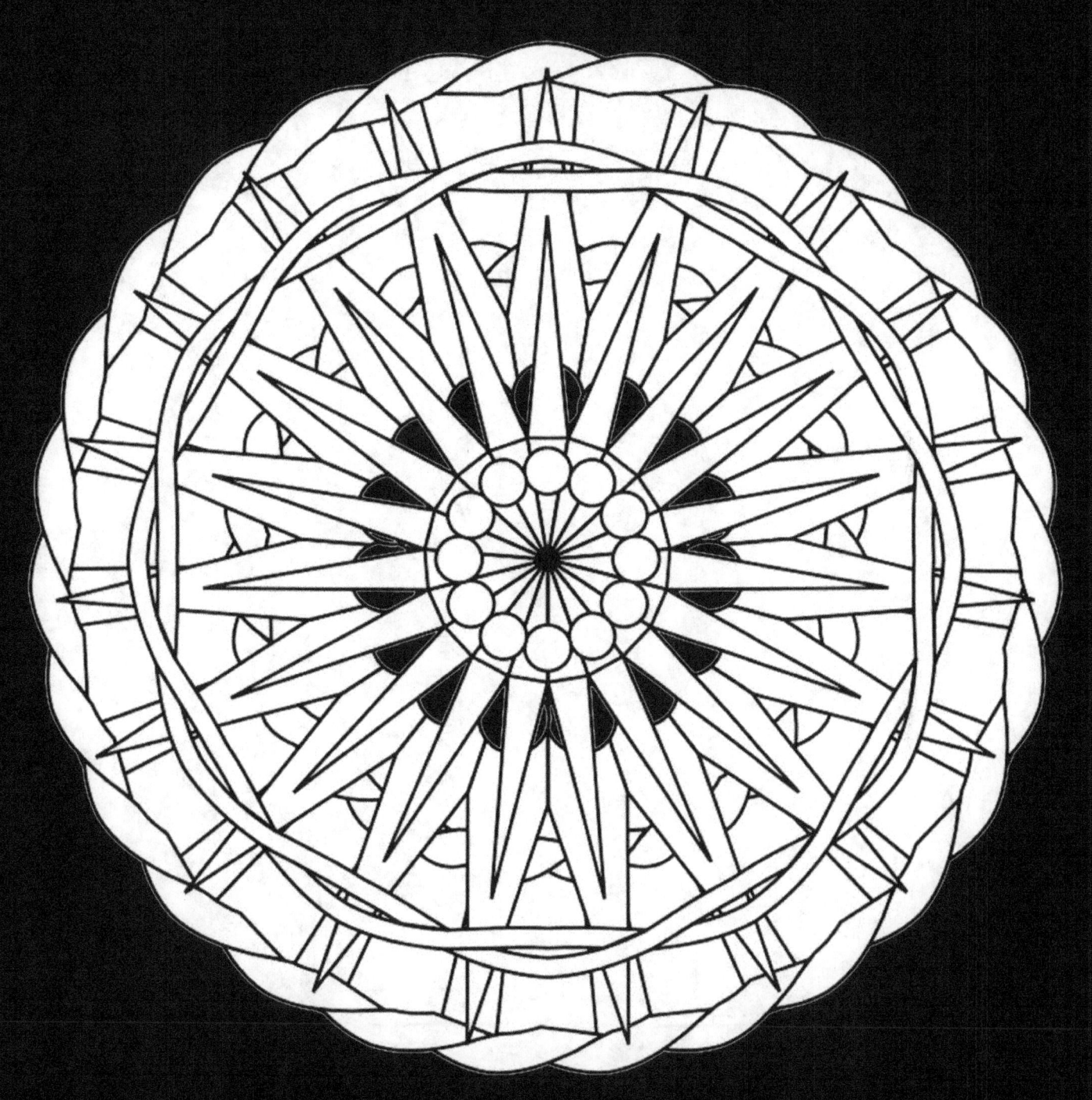

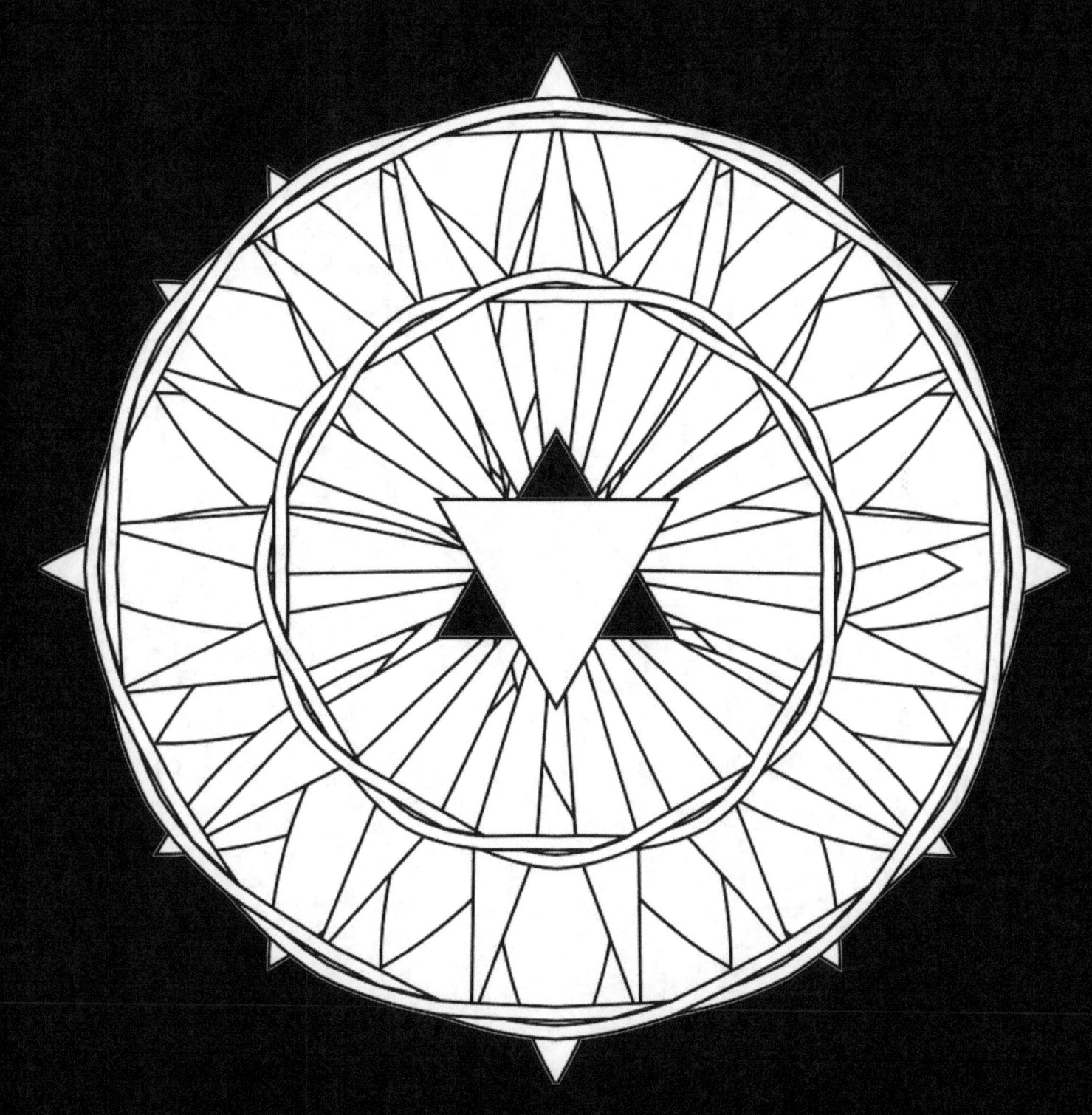

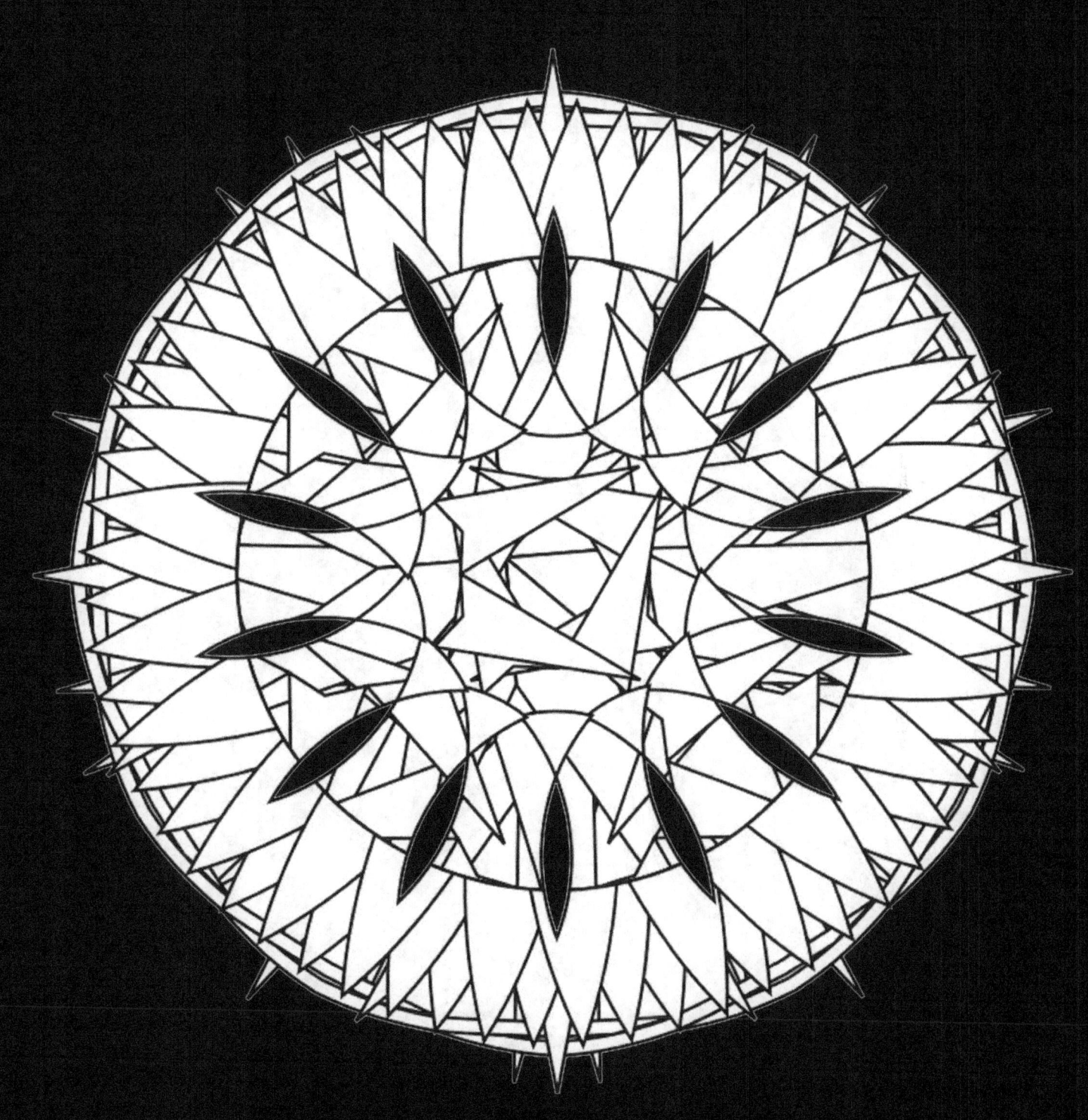

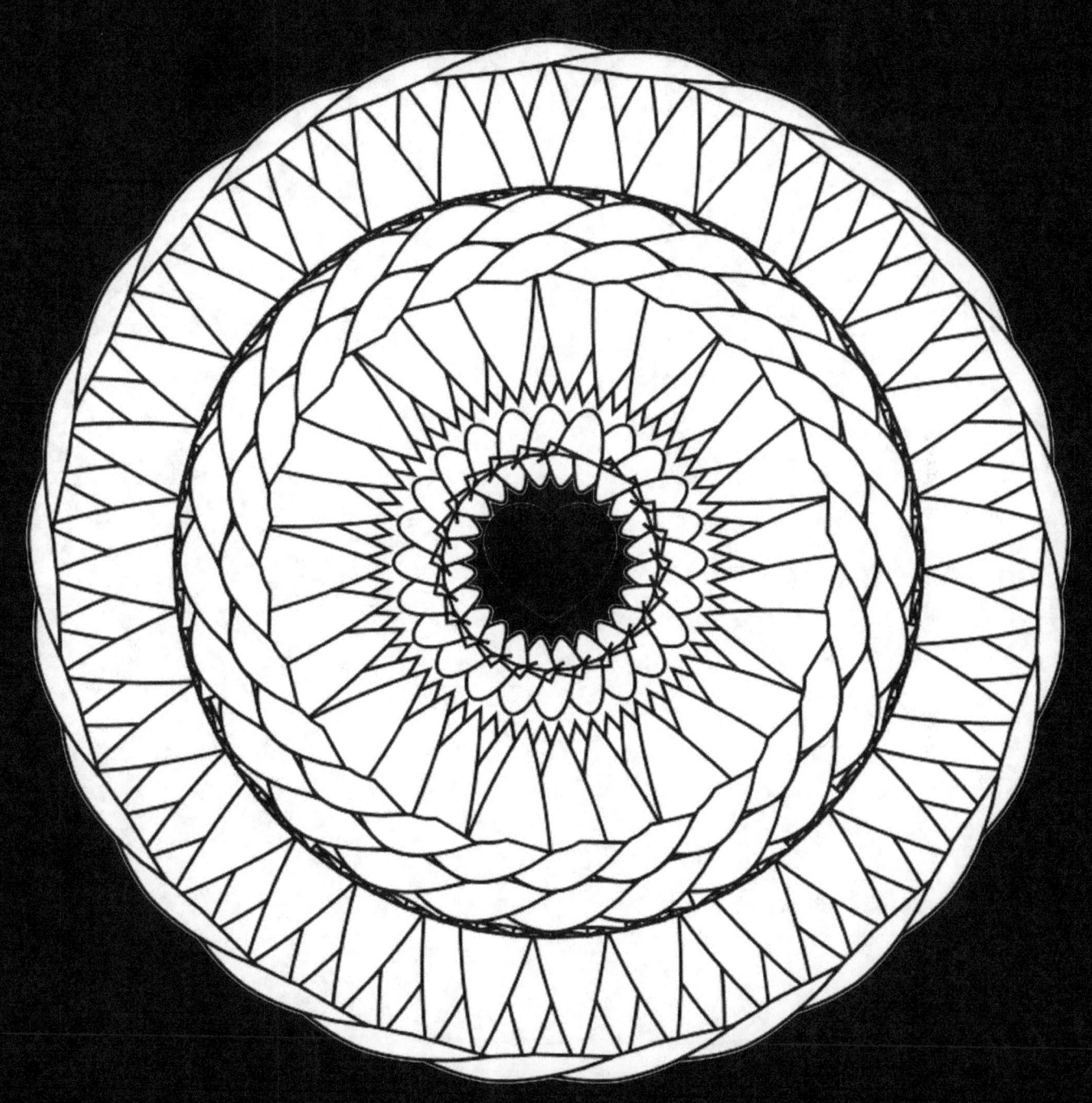

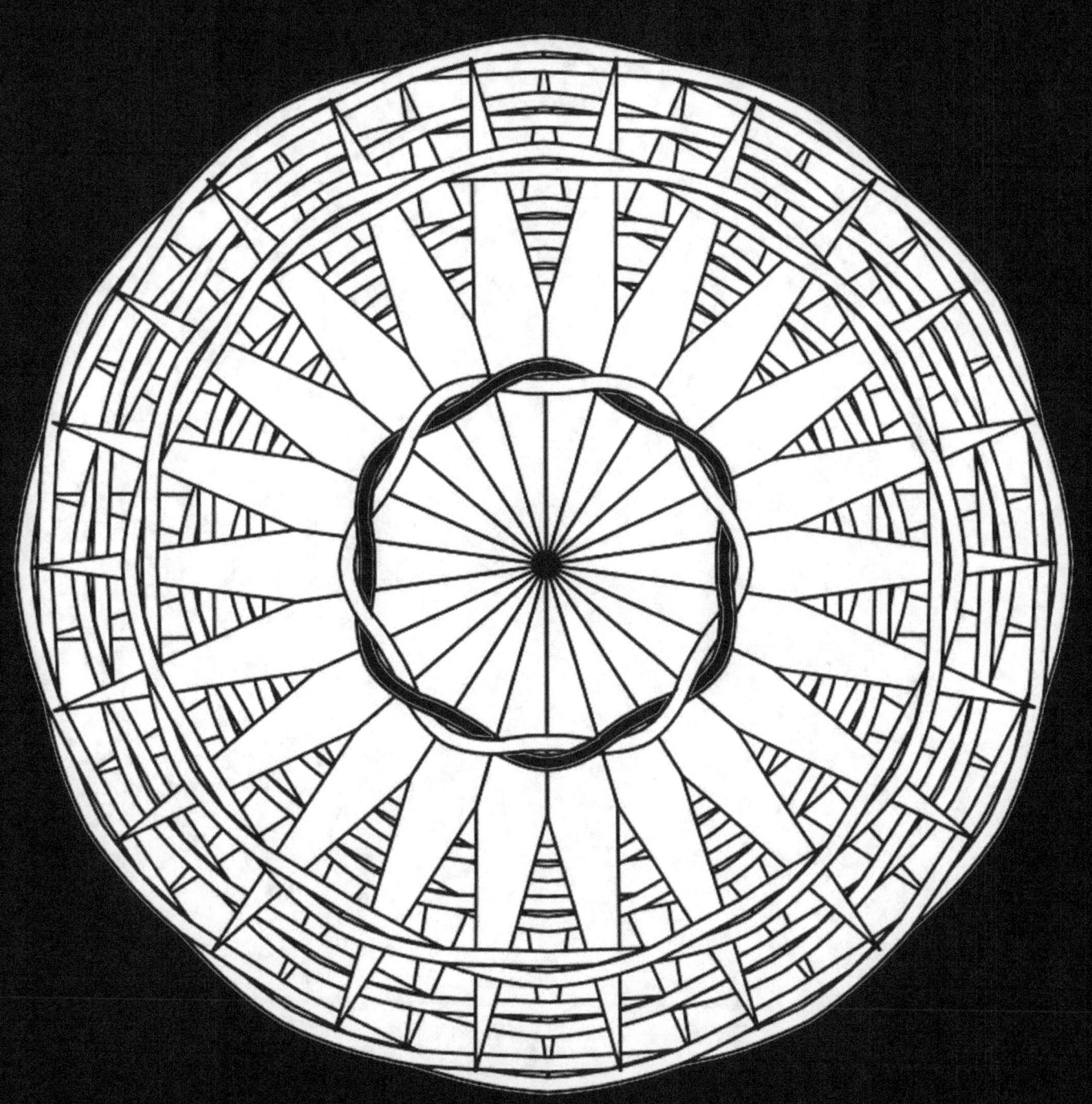

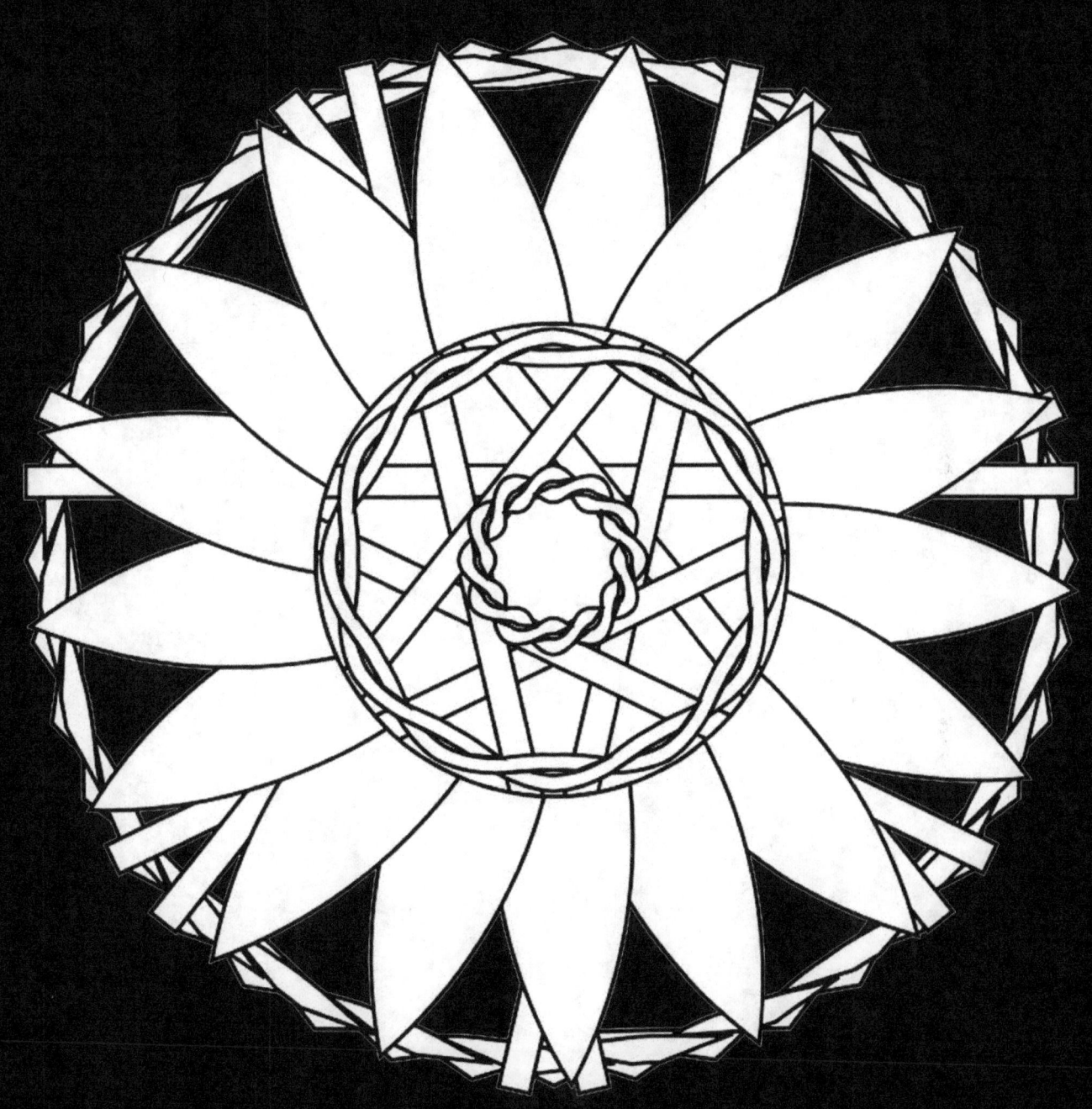

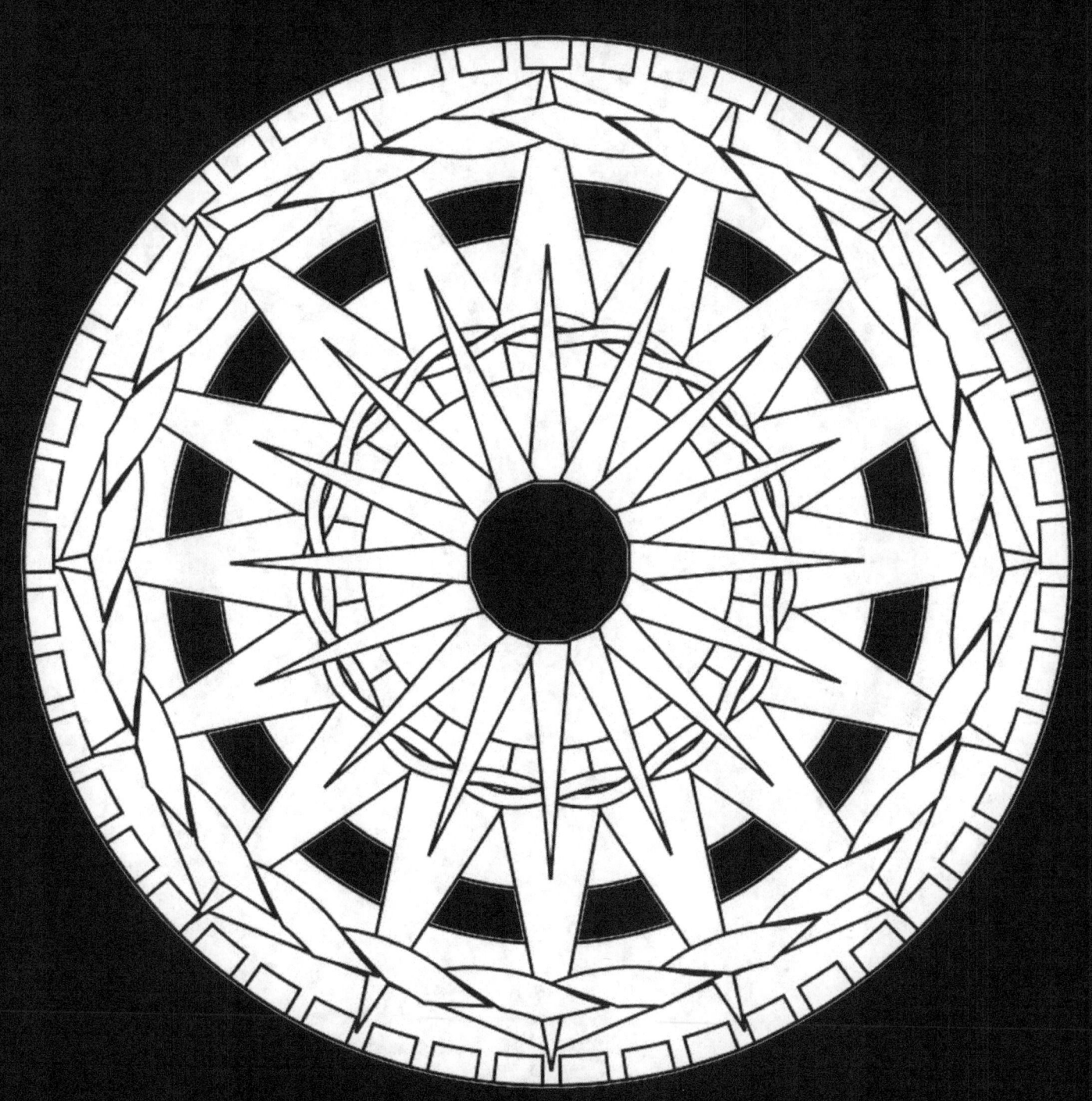

Other Coloring Books by
Vincent Van Gouache

All available from Amazon

Psycho Color

Psycho Color 2

Mandala Mania

The Psycho Color Collection

The Book of Calm

Relax

Creative Coloring - 100 Mandalas

Warrior Shields

Midnight Mandala Mania